"CHICKENS" BY MORI ŌGAI

Japanese "Characters"

A COLLECTION OF GRADED READERS
FOR STUDENTS OF JAPANESE

ELEMENTARY

1 Stories by Teramura Teruo (1992)

INTERMEDIATE

4 Stories by Tsubota Jōji (1992)

ADVANCED

9 "Chickens" by Mori Ōgai (1992)

Japanese "Characters"
GRADED READERS: INTERMEDIATE

9

"Chickens" by Mori Ōgai

translated by

Edmund R. Skrzypczak

JAPAN PUBLICATIONS TRADING CO., LTD.
TOKYO, JAPAN

Published by JAPAN PUBLICATIONS TRADING CO., LTD.
1-2-1, Sarugaku-chō, Chiyoda-ku,
Tokyo, 101 Japan

Distributors:

UNITED STATES & CANADA: *JP Trading, Inc., P. O. BOX 610, 300 Industrial Way, Brisbane, CA 94005.*

BRITISH ISLES & EUROPEAN CONTINENT: *Premier Book Marketing Ltd., 1 Gower Street, London WC1E 6HA.*

AUSTRALIA & NEW ZEALAND: *Bookwise International, 54 Crittenden Road, Findon, South Australia 5023.*

THE FAR EAST & JAPAN: *Japan Publications Trading Co., Ltd., 1-2-1, Sarugaku-chō, Chiyoda-ku, Tokyo, 101 Japan.*

First edition: July 1992 (First printing)

ISBN 0-87040-916-6

Printed in Japan

Contents

7   *About the Series*

11   Introduction

15   "Chickens"

About the Series

*T*ens of thousands of people around the world are now studying Japanese as a foreign language. University departments that offer Japanese are experiencing an unprecedented boom. Japanese is being taught in more and more high schools, and even in primary schools in some parts of the world.

Regardless of their ages, there comes a point when these language students would like to read something in Japanese. If they are beginners, or sometimes even if they have been studying Japanese for two or three years, they still do not know enough kanji to be able to read ordinary books in Japanese. Or, even if the book is mostly in kana, they find the vocabulary too much of a problem. Thus, whether it be kanji that is the obstacle, or vocabulary, their desire to read is frustrated.

The books in this series are designed to meet the needs of such students. They will bridge the gap between the classroom and the library (or bookshop). They will also, I believe, help students consolidate what they learn in the classroom, because stories about situations that can be easily imagined provide tangible examples of words, phrases, and grammatical structures being used in specific contexts. These examples leave deep impressions on the imagination and memory of the reader.

I have tried as much as possible to make the English translation pass muster as English. More important to me, however, was capturing the sense and feeling of the original Japanese, since the idea of having a translation opposite the Japanese text is to aid the student to understand the original. Sometimes capturing the sense of the original meant choosing an English turn of expression that is far from a literal translation of the Japanese, yet is what would be (or could be) used in English to convey the same meaning. After all, the expression, the communication, of meaning is what language is all about, and the reader should learn to grasp the meaning of what is being read.

It is always a problem when devising a series of books such as this, to imagine who the readers will be. Will they be university students? high-school students? second-year students of the language? third-year students? Et cetera. At first I planned to assume that the potential reader would have studied Japanese for two years using one of Anthony Alfonso's structured textbooks, because then I would know, roughly, what vocabulary, grammar, and kanji the reader would have learned. But in view of the enormous boom in Japanese language study in recent years, with the subsequent proliferation of textbooks and diversity in teaching approaches, I decided to aim at a very vague type of reader: someone who had learned some Japanese (formally or informally), knew enough kana to get started, and maybe knew no kanji whatsoever—but who wanted something to read.

For this reason, the first book in this series begins with very few kanji, which appear with the kana readings over them. In subsequent books kanji are introduced more frequently, but in such a way as not, I trust, to overburden the reader. The series as a whole will be divided into three levels of difficulty: elementary, intermediate, and advanced, with the number of kanji increasing gradually with each book in the series.

The Japanese stories chosen for inclusion in this series have been selected because they show aspects of Japan or of Japanese people — sometimes even aspects of the authors who wrote the stories — that reveal the Japanese as people. This is important, because the whole key to understanding people of other countries is the realization that, underneath their different appearances and different ways of doing things, they are people, the same as you, the same as the other people you know.

Finally, the stories were also chosen in the hope that they will prove entertaining. This can be a difficult order to fill sometimes, since what is entertaining to me might not be so to everyone else. Still, most people enjoy meeting interesting people, and it is with this in mind that I have aimed at introducing you to some real "characters." Happy reading!

Edmund R. Skrzypczak

Introduction

The author of the story in this book, Mori Ōgai, is a famous figure in Japanese literature. He was born in 1862 in Tsuwano in present-day Shimane Prefecture, the son of a doctor of high standing in the Tsuwano clan. His serious education began early (at the age of 5), and after he had learned all there was to be learned in his part of the country, his father sent him to Tokyo for further studies. He was too young to enter Tokyo University, but his father doctored his birth certificate to make him two years older, and he thus successfully entered the Medical Faculty of that university. He graduated from there in July 1881 — at the age of 20! He entered the Japanese army as a doctor in December of that same year. Because he was intellectually gifted, the army sent him to Germany to study the science of hygiene, which he studied at several universities in Germany for four years. He returned to Japan in 1888, full of knowledge about hygiene, and about European ways as well.

The next ten or eleven years were years filled with frustration, as he battled with army superiors and The Establishment in the medical profession. They were not as ready to make the kind of changes in medical practices, or even hygienic practices, that he so eagerly proposed. They had sent him to Europe to learn the new ways, but they were not too willing to change to the new ways when he suggested them. Finally, to move him out of Tokyo, where he was making a name for himself, his army superiors transferred him to a town in Kyushu called Kokura, appointing him head of the 12th Medical Corps. There he remained posted until 1902, when he was reassigned to Tokyo, and shortly thereafter he was named the director of the Bureau of Medical Affairs in the Ministry of War.

The story in this book was published in 1909, but it is about his days in Kokura approximately ten years earlier. In the story you will, I hope, get some insight into the type of character Mori Ōgai was, as you read about an officer in the Japanese army who somehow does not fit the image one normally has of a Japanese army officer. Here, for example, we meet an officer who does almost anything he can to *avoid* a battle.

Some of the kanji that appear in this story are no longer used. Indeed, a few of the words are no longer used, either. As regards the choice of words, I have not replaced any obsolete words with modern words, out of respect for a writer of Mori Ōgai's stature. As regards kanji, though, I have ventured to replace some old forms of kanji with new forms, or to replace some kanji with hiragana, in accord with the normal prac-

kanji with hiragana, in accord with the normal practice of publishers of modern versions of older works.

The reading on this level may be quite difficult, but I trust you will not mind the extra effort, if it has enabled you to become acquainted with another interesting Japanese character: in this case, Mori Ōgai himself.

Chickens

MORI Ōgai

鶏

石田小介が少佐参謀になって小倉に着任したのは六月二十四日であった。

徳山と門司との間を交通している蒸気船から上がったのが午前三時である。地方の軍隊は送迎がなかなか手厚いことを知っていたから、石田はその頃の通常礼装というのをして、勲章をおびていた。古参の大尉参謀が同僚を代表して桟橋まで来ていた。

雨がどっどと降っている。これから小倉までは汽車で一時間は掛からない。川卯という家で飯を焚かせて食う。夜が明けてから、大尉は走り迴って、切符の世話やら荷物の世話やらしてくれる。

汽車の窓からは、崖の上にぴっしり立て並べてある小家が見える。どの家も戸を開け放して、女や子供が殆ど裸でいる。中には丁度朝飯を食っている家もある。仲仕のような仕事をする労働者の家だと士官が話して聞せた。

田圃の中に出る。稲の植附けはもう済んでいる。おり

Chickens

It was 24 June when Ishida Shōsuke, newly promoted to staff major, arrived to take up his new post in Kokura.

He had come off the steamboat that runs between Tokuyama and Moji at 3:00 that morning. Since he knew that the army personnel in remote areas gave very warm receptions, he had worn the dress uniform of the season, complete with medals. The senior Staff Captain, representing his fellow officers, was at the pier to meet him.

It was pouring rain. From Moji to Kokura would take less than an hour by train. They had a meal prepared for them at an inn called "Kawau." After it was light outside, the captain rushed about and took care of the tickets, baggage, and whatever else had to be done.

From the window of the train he saw shanties jammed one against the other atop the escarpment alongside the tracks. All the dwellings had their doors open; the women and children had almost nothing on. Some of the families were in the middle of their breakfast. These were the dwellings of laborers — dock workers, for example — explained an officer.

They passed through rice fields. Planting of the rice shoots was already completed. From time to time a

おり蓑を着て手篭を担いで畔道をあるいている農夫が見える。

段々小倉が近くなってくる。最初に見える人家は旭町の遊廓である。どの家にも二階の欄干に赤い布団が掛けてある。こんな日に干すのでもあるまい。毎日降るのだから、こうして曝すのであろう。

がらがらと音がして、汽車が紫川の鉄道橋を渡ると、間もなく小倉の停車場に着く。参謀長を始め、大勢の出迎人がある。一同にそこそこに挨拶をして、室町の達見という宿屋にはいった。

隊から来ている従卒に手伝って貰って、石田は早速正装に着更えて司令部へ出た。その頃は申告の仕方なんぞは決まっていなかったが、廉あって上官に謁する時というので、着任の挨拶は正装ですることになっていた。

翌日も雨が降っている。鍛治町に借家があるというのを見に行く。砂地であるのに、道普請に石炭屑を使うので、薄墨色の水が町を流れている。

借家は町の南側になっている。生垣で囲んだ、相応な屋敷である。庭には石炭屑を敷かないので、奇麗な砂が降るだけの雨を皆吸込んで、濡れたとも見えずにいる。

farmer appeared, walking along a path between pad-
dies, wearing a straw raincoat and shouldering a pole
with a pair of night-soil buckets balanced on the ends.

They were approaching Kokura. The first dwellings he saw were the licensed quarters in Asahi-machi.
All the houses had red sleeping quilts hanging over the
upper-story railings. They couldn't possibly be drying
them on a day like this, he thought; since it rains every
day, they must just be airing them.

The train clattered across the Murasaki River rail-
way bridge; soon after, it arrived at Kokura's main sta-
tion. A huge welcoming party was waiting, led by the
Chief of Staff. After brief greetings to those assembled,
Ishida entered a lodging house in Muro-machi called
"Tatsumi."

Helped by an orderly assigned to him from the
company, he promptly changed to a full-dress uniform
and went to headquarters. In those days there was no
fixed way of reporting to a superior, but since it was
considered a formal meeting with a higher officer, it
was customary for a new arrival to wear full-dress uniform when paying this courtesy call.

It was raining the next day, too. He went to look at
a house for rent in Kaji-machi. Though the ground was
a sandy soil, gray-black rivulets flowed through the
streets because of the coal tailings they used for repairing the roadways.

The house for rent was on the south side of Kaji-
machi. It was quite a large residence, enclosed by a
hedge. Because there were no coal tailings laid down in
the garden, the clean sand sucked up whatever rain fell
and so did not look the slightest bit wet.

眞中に大きな百日紅の木がある。垣の方に寄って夾竹桃が五六本立っている。

車から降りるのを見ていたと見えて、家主が出て来て案内をする。澁紙色の顔をした、萎びた爺さんである。石田は防水布の雨覆いを脱いで、門口を這入って、脱いだ雨覆いを裏返して巻いて縁端に置こうとすると、爺さんが手に取った。石田は縁を濡らさない用心かと思いながら、爺さんの顔を見た。爺さんは言訣のように、この辺は往来から見える所に物を置くのは危険だということを話した。石田が長靴を脱ぐと、爺さんは長靴も一しょに持って先に立った。

石田は爺さんに案内せられて家を見た。この土地の家は大小の違があるばかりで、どの家も皆同じ平面図に依って建てたように出来ている。門口を入って左側が外壁で、家は右の方へ長方形に延びている。その長方形が表側と裏側に分かれていて、裏側が勝手になっているのである。

東京から来た石田の目には、先づ柱が鐵丹か何かで、代赭のような色に塗ってあるのが異様に感ぜられた。併し不快だとも思わない。唯この家なんぞは建ててから余り年数を経たものではないらしいのに、何となく古い、

A large crepe myrtle stood in the very middle of the garden. Nearer the hedge fence stood a half dozen or so sweet oleanders.

Apparently the owner of the house had been watching Ishida get out of the rickshaw, for he came out to greet him. He was a shriveled old man with a light-brown complexion.

Ishida removed his oilskin raincoat and stepped through the front gate. Turning the raincoat inside out and rolling it into a bundle, he made a move to place it on the edge of the verandah, when the old man took it from him. Wondering if this was a precaution so the verandah did not get wet, Ishida looked quizzically at him. By way of explanation, the old man said that in that neighborhood it was dangerous to leave anything where it could be seen from the street. When Ishida removed his boots, the old man took them along, too, and led the way inside.

He then gave Ishida a tour of the house. Houses in this region differed only in size; they were all constructed according to the same floor plan. As you came through the front gate, on your left was the outer wall, with the house itself extending to the right in a rectangular shape. This rectangle was divided into a front half and a back half, the back half being the kitchen area.

The first thing that struck the eyes of someone from Tokyo like Ishida as being different was the way the pillars were colored a burnt sienna with red oxide or something. Not that he found it unpleasant. But although the house seemed to have been built not very many years before, it gave an indefinable impression of

時代のある家のように思われる。それでこんな家に住んでいたら、気が落ち付くだろうというような心持がした。

表側は、玄関から次の間を経て、右に突き当たる西の詰めが一番好い座敷で、床の間が附いている。爺さんは「一寸御免なさい」と言って、勝手へ往ったが、外套と靴とを置いて、座布団と烟草盆とを持って出て来た。そうして百日紅の植わっている庭の方の雨戸が疎らに締まっているのを、がらがらと繰り開けた。庭は内から見れば、割合に広い。爺さんは生垣を指ざして、この辺は要塞が近いので石塀や煉瓦塀を築くことはやかましいが、表だけは立派にしたいと思って問い合わせて見たら、低い塀は築いても好いそうだから、その内都合をしてどうかしようと思っていると話した。

表通は中くらいの横町で、向いの平家の低い窓が生垣の透間から見える。窓には竹簾が掛けてある。その中で糸を引いている音がぶうんぶうんとねむたそうに聞こえている。

石田は座布団を敷居の上に敷いて、柱に寄り掛かって膝を立てて、ポケットから金天狗を出して一本吸い附けた。爺さんは縁端にしゃがんで何か言っていたが、いつ

age, of having been in existence for generations. Hence he had the feeling he would feel very much at home living in a house like this.

In the front half, from the entranceway you passed an anteroom on your right and came to the western corner-room; it was the best sitting room in the house, complete with tokonoma. The old man excused himself for a minute and went to the kitchen, where he left the raincoat and boots, and re-appeared with a cushion to sit on and a bowl for smoking. Then with a loud clatter he shoved open the partially closed shutters on the side facing the garden where the crepe myrtle was growing. Seen from inside, the garden was quite large. Pointing to the hedge fence, the old man told him that the authorities were strict against the putting up of stone or brick walls in this neighborhood because the fort was nearby, but, wanting to give the front of the house, at least, a nice appearance, he had made enquiries and they said he could put a low wall up, so he was planning to have something done about it one of these days.

The street in front was a medium-sized alley. Through openings in the hedge could be seen the low windows of the one-story house across the street. Bamboo blinds were hung across the windows. From inside the house came the sleepy humming sound of a spinning wheel at work.

Ishida placed the cushion across the shutter sill; leaning against the pillar, he drew up his legs, took a Kintengu cigar from his pocket, and lit it. The old man was squatting on the edge of the verandah, talking away. Somewhere along the line the topic shifted from

か家の話が家賃の話になり、家賃の話が身の上話になった。この薄井という爺さんは夫婦で西隣に住んでいる。遅く出来た息子が豊津の中学に入れてある。この家を人に貸して、暮らしを立てて倅の学費を出さねばならないということである。

　それから裏側の方の間取を見た。こちらは西の詰めが小さい間になっている。その次がやや広い。この二間が表側の床の間のある座敷の裏になっている。表側の次の間と玄関との裏が、半ば土間になっている台所である。井戸は土間の隅に掘ってある。

　縁側に出て見れば、裏庭は表庭の三倍位の広さである。所々に蜜柑の木があって、小さい実が沢山生っている。縁に近い所には、瓦で築いた花壇があって、菊が造ってある。その傍に丸石を畳んだ井戸があって、どの石の隙間からも赤い蟹が覗いている。花壇の向こうは畑になっていて、その西の隅に別当部屋の附いた厠がある。花壇の上にも、畑の上にも、蜜柑の木の周囲にも、蜜蜂が沢山飛んでいるので、石田は大そう蜜蜂の多い所だと思って爺さんに問うて見た。これは爺さんが飼っているので、巣は東側の外壁に弔り下げてあるのであった。

the house to the rent, then from the rent to personal details. The old fellow, Usui by name, was living with his wife next door, on the western side. A son born to them late in life was being sent to a junior high school in Toyotsu. They had to lease this house in order to make a living and pay their son's school expenses.

Next they looked at the room arrangements in the back half of the house. The western corner-room in the back was a small room. The one next to it was a bit bigger. These two rooms corresponded to the sitting room with tokonoma on the front side. Corresponding to the anteroom and entranceway on the front was the kitchen, half of it a sunken earth-floor. A well had been sunk in one corner of the earth-floor area.

Stepping out onto the verandah, Ishida found the back garden was three times as big as the front one. There were a few mandarin trees about, each laden with a large number of small fruit. Near the verandah there was a flower bed built up with roof tiles; it had a display of chrysanthemums. Beside it was a well constructed of layers of round stones; red crabs peeped out from every chink between the rocks. On the far side of the flower bed was a vegetable garden, at the western corner of which was a stable with an attached room for the stableman. There were so many bees flying about in the flower bed, in the vegetable garden, and around the mandarin trees that Ishida felt the place had an unusually large number of them, and he asked the old man about this. It turned out the old man was keeping them; their hive was hanging from the outer wall on the eastern side of the property.

　石田はこれだけ見て、いったん爺さんに別れて帰ったが、家はかなり気に入ったので、宿屋のお上さんに頼んで、細かい事を取り決めて貰って、二三日たって引っ越した。

　横浜から船に載せた馬も着いていたので、別当に引き入れさせた。

　勝手道具を買う。膳椀を買う。蚊帳を買う。買いに行くのは従卒の島村である。

　家主はまめな爺さんで、来ていろいろ世話を焼いてくれる。膳椀を買うとき、爺さんが問うた。

「何人前入りまするかの。」

「二人前です。」

「下のもののは入りませんかの。」

「僕のと下女のとで二人前です。従卒は隊で食います、別当も自分で遣るのです。」

　蚊帳は自分のと下女のと別当のと三張買った。その時も爺さんが問うた。

「布団は入りませんかの。」

「毛布があります。」

　万事こんな風である。それでも五十円程掛かった。

　女中を雇うというので、宿屋の達見のお上さんが口入

Having seen this much, Ishida bade farewell to the old man and returned to his lodgings; since the house had quite captured his fancy, he asked the landlady to handle the fine details for him, and a few days later he moved.

His horse, sent by ship from Yokohama, had arrived in the meantime, so he had the stableman bring it in.

There were kitchen utensils to buy. Dishes for the table to buy. Mosquito nets to buy. The one doing the buying was to be the orderly, Shimamura.

The landlord, helpful old man that he was, came over and sought to be of assistance in a variety of ways—some of them unwanted. When Ishida was ordering the dishes for the table, the old man queried:

"How many settings do you want?"

"For two."

"Won't you need some for the servants?"

"One set for me and one for the housemaid makes two settings. The orderly eats at the camp. And the stableman will take care of himself."

He ordered three mosquito nets: his, the housemaid's, and the stableman's. Again the old man queried:

"Won't you need any quilts?"

"There are blankets."

Everything was kept to a minimum this way. Even so, it added up to a shocking fifty yen.

He notified the landlady at his earlier lodgings, the "Tatsumi," that he wished to hire a maidservant, and she sent a woman who ran an employment service over

屋の上さんをよこしてくれた。石田は婆さんを置きたいという注文をした。時という五十ばかりの婆さんが来た。夫婦で小学校の教員の弁当をこしらえているもので、その婆さんの方が来てくれたのだそうだ。不思議に喋らない。黙って台所をしてくれる。

　二三日立った。毎日雨は降ったり止んだりしている。石田は雨覆いをはおって馬で司令部にでる。東京から新たに雇って来た別当の虎吉が、始めて伴をするとき、こう言った。

「旦那。馬の合羽がありませんがなあ。」

「有る。」

「ええ。それは鞍丈にかぶせる小さい奴ならあります。旦那の膝に掛けるのがありません。」

「そんなものは入らない。」

「それでもお膝が濡れます。どこの旦那も持っています。」

「膝なんざあ濡れてもいい。馬装に膝かけなんというものはない。外の人は持っておっても、己は入らない。」

「へへへへ。それでは野木さんのお流儀で。」*

「己が入らないのだ。野木閣下の事はどうか知らん。」

「へえ。」

to meet him. Ishida indicated a desire to have an elderly woman who would stay in. Later, an old woman of fifty, Toki by name, arrived. He was to learn from others that she and her husband were making lunchbox meals for the teachers at the primary schools, and she had agreed to come and work for him. She was strangely taciturn. She would do her kitchen work without saying a word.

A few days passed. It rained on and off every day. Ishida went to headquarters on horseback, a rain cloak over his uniform. The first time the new stableman from Tokyo, Torakichi, accompanied him, he said:

"Master, we need an oilskin for the horse."

"We have one."

"Yes, we do have a small one that covers the saddle only. What we need is one to put over Master's knees."

"We need nothing of the sort!"

"But Master's knees will get wet. Every other master has one."

"My knees can get wet, for all I care. A lap rug is not a standard part of riding gear. Other people may have them, but I will do without."

"Heh heh heh heh. Following Lord Nogi's example, eh?"

"I'm speaking only of my own wishes. I don't know about His Excellency Lord Nogi."

"Yessir."

---

* Nogi Maresuke (1849–1912), general in the Japanese army and recipient of various titles of nobility from the Meiji emperor, was much admired by Mori Ōgai for his devotion to the "traditional" values of discipline, self-sacrifice, austerity, and patriotism.

その後は別当も敢て言わない。

石田は司令部から引掛に、師団長はじめ上官の家に名刺を出す。その頃は都督がおられたので、それへも名刺を出す。中には面会せられる方もある。家へ帰って見ると、部下のものが名刺を置きに来るので、いつでも二三枚づつはある。商人が手土産なんぞを置いて帰ったのもある。そうすると、石田はすぐに島村に持たせて返しに遣る。それだから、島村は物を貰うのを苦に病んでいて、自分のいる時に持って来たのは大抵受け取らない。

ある日帰って見ると、島村と押し問答をしているものがある。相手は百姓らしい風体の男である。見れば鶏の生きたのを一羽持っている。その男が、石田を見ると、にこにこして傍へ寄って来て、こう言った。

「少佐殿。お見忘れになりましたか知れませんが、戦地でお世話になった輜重輸卒の麻生でござります。」

「うむ。軍司令部にいた麻生か。」

「はい。」

「どうして来た。」

「予備役になりまして帰っております。内は大里でござります。少佐殿におなりになって、こちらへお出だということを聞きましたので、御機嫌伺に参りました。これ

The stableman never ventured to bring the subject up again.

After leaving headquarters Ishida would present his name card at the houses of his superior officers, beginning with the Division Commander's. Because the Governor-General was there at the time, he presented a name card at his place, too. With some of them he had to spend some time in a visit. When he returned home he would find some of his subordinates had come to leave their name cards, and every day there would be two or three cards. Sometimes there also were gifts of one kind or another left by merchants. In such cases Ishida immediately sent Shimamura to return the articles. For this reason Shimamura dreaded their receiving anything, and he almost always refused to accept anything brought while he was there.

One day Ishida returned home to find someone engaged in a tug of words with Shimamura. The fellow looked like a farmer. He was holding a live chicken in his arms. When the fellow saw Ishida, he approached him, all smiles, and said:

"Major, sir! You may not remember my face, but you took care of me at the front. I am Supply Infantry-man Asō."

"Ah yes, the Asō who was in army headquarters?"

"Yes, sir."

"What are you doing here?"

"I was placed on the reserve list and sent home. I live in Dairi, near here. I heard you were made a major and were posted here, so I called to pay my respects.

は沢山飼っております内の一羽でござりますが、丁度好い頃のでござりますから、持って上がりました。」

「ふむ。立派な鳥だなあ。それは徴発ではあるまいな。」

麻生は五分刈りの頭を搔いた。

「恐れ入ります。ついみんなが徴発徴発と申すもんでござりますから、ああいうことを申しましてお叱りを受けました。」

「それでも貴様はあれ切り、支那人の物を取らんようになったから感心だ。」

「全くお陰を持ちまして心得違いを致しませんものですから、凱旋いたしますまで、どの位肩身が広がったか知れません。大連で皆が背囊を調べられましたときも、銀の簪が出たり、女の着物が出たりして恥を搔く中で、わたくしだけは大威張りでござりました。あの金州の鶏なんぞは、ちゃんが、ほい、又お叱りを受け損なう所でござりました、支那人が逃げた跡に、卵を抱いていたので、主はないのだと申しますのに、そんならその主のない家に持って行って置いて来いとおっしゃったのには、実におどろきましたのでござります。」

「ははは。己は頑固だからなあ。」

「どう致しまして。あれはわたくしの一生の教訓になり

This is one of many birds we have; it's in its prime right now, so I brought it for you."

"Hmm. A beautiful bird, that one. It wouldn't by any chance be something that you *requisitioned*, would it?"

Asō scratched his close-cropped head. "I'm still ashamed of that incident. Everyone was saying 'Requisition,' 'Requisition,' so before I knew it I was doing the same thing — and got a reprimand from you."

"Even so, I had to admire the way you stopped taking things from the Chinese after that."

"Certainly thanks to you I was not guilty of any further lapses, and I can't tell you how proud I was when I returned at the end of the war. When everyone's backpacks were searched in Dairen, they turned up silver hairpins and women's garments and things, much to everyone else's shame, but I was the only one who could hold his chest up high. Then there was that chicken in Chinchow. After the Chinks — sorry, I was almost going to get a reprimand from you again — I mean, after the Chinese fled, there it was, brooding on eggs and without an owner, but when I explained this to you your answer was, 'In that case, take it back to its ownerless house and leave it there!' You can't imagine how surprised I was."

"Ha ha ha ha! I'm very bull-headed, aren't I?"

"Not at all. That was a lesson to me for the rest of

ましたのでござりました。もうお暇を致します。」

「泊まって行かんか。己の内は戦地と同じで御馳走はないが。」

「奥様はいらっしゃりませんか。」

「妻はこないだ死んだ。」

「へえ。それはどうも。」

「島村が知っているが、まるで戦地のような暮らしを遣っているのだ。」

「それは御不自由でいらっしゃりましょう。詰まらないことを申し上げて、お召替のお邪魔を致しました。これでお暇を致します。」

　麻生は鶏を島村に渡して、鞋をびちゃびちゃ言わせて帰って行った。

　石田は長靴を脱いで上がる。雨覆いを脱いで島村にわたす。島村は雨覆いと靴を持って勝手へ行く。石田は西の詰めの間に入って、床の間の前に行って、帽をそこに据えてある将校行李の上に置く。軍刀を床の間に横に置く。これを初めて来た日に、お時婆さんが床の間の壁に立て掛けて、叱られたのである。立てた物は倒れることがある。倒れれば刀が傷む。壁にも傷が付くかも知れないというのである。

my life . . . . I'll take my leave of you now."

"Why don't you stay the night? There won't be anything special — we eat here same as they do on the front, but still . . . ."

"Isn't the Mrs with you?"

"My wife died some time ago."

"Oh. I'm sorry . . . ."

"As Shimamura here can tell you, I'm living exactly as I would on the battlefield."

"Then you must be putting up with a few inconveniences. Here, I've kept you from changing with all this silly talk of mine. I'll take my leave of you now."

Asō handed the chicken to Shimamura and pitter-pattered off on his straw sandals.

Ishida removed his boots and stepped into the house. He took off his rain cloak and handed it to Shimamura. The latter carried the cloak and the boots to the kitchen area. Ishida entered the western corner-room, went to the tokonoma, and put his cap on top of the officer's traveling case placed there. He put his sabre down flat inside the tokonoma. The old lady, Toki, had been reprimanded about this on the first day she came, when she stood it up against the wall of the tokonoma. "Things that are stood up sometimes fall over. If the sabre falls over the blade will get damaged. The wall might get scratched, too," he had told her.

　床の間の前には、子供が手習に使うような机が据えてある。その前に毛布が畳んで敷いてある。石田は夏衣袴のままで毛布の上に胡坐を搔いた。そこへ勝手から婆さんが出て来た。

「鳥はどうしなさりまするかの。」

「飯の菜がないのか。」

「茄子に隠元豆が煮えておりまするが。」

「それで好い。」

「鳥は。」

「鳥は生かして置け。」

「はい。」

　婆さんは腹の中で、相変らずけちな人だと思った。この婆さんの観察した所では、石田に二つの性質がある。一つはけちである。肴は長浜の女が盤台を頭の上に載せて売りに来るのであるが、まだ小鯛を一度しか買わない。野菜が旨いというので、胡瓜や茄子ばかり食っている。酒は丸で呑まない。菓子は一度買って来いと言われて、名物の鶴の子を買って来た所が、「まずいなあ」と言いながら皆平らげてしまって、それ切買って来いとは言わない。今一つは馬鹿だということである。物の値段が分らない。いくらと言っても黙って払う。人が土産を持っ

In front of the tokonoma there had been placed the kind of desk children use for writing practice. In front of the desk lay a folded blanket. Still in his summer uniform, Ishida sat cross-legged on the blanket. Just as he sat down, the old lady came out from the kitchen.

"What do you wish to do with the bird?"

"Have you got something to go with the rice?"

"There's eggplant, and I'm boiling some kidney beans."

"That'll be fine."

"What about the bird?"

"Let it stay alive."

"Yes, sir."

In her heart the old woman thought, "As stingy as ever!" From what she had observed of him already, he had two main tendencies. One was to be stingy. Take fish, for example. A woman comes from Nagahama with a basket of fresh fish on her head for sale, and so far he's bought only one small sea bream, once. He says he likes vegetables, and so all he ever eats are cucumbers and eggplants. He doesn't touch a drop of sake. And sweets—told one time to buy some, she had brought back the local speciality, "Crane Eggs," but he kept remarking how awful they were as he finished them all off, and he's never told her to buy any sweets again. The other main tendency was to be a fool. He didn't have any idea of prices. Whatever price was asked he would pay it without saying a word. When people brought

てくるのを一々返しに遣る。婆さんは先ずこれだけの観察をしているのである。

　婆さんが立つとき、石田は「湯が取ってあるか」と言った。「はい」と言って、婆さんは勝手へ引込んだ。

　石田は、裏側の詰めの間に出る。ここには水指とうがい茶碗と湯を取った金だらいとバケツとが置いてある。これは初の日から決めてあるので、朝晩とも同じである。

　石田は先ず楊枝を使う。うがいをする。湯で顔を洗う。石鹸は七十銭位の舶来品を使っている。何故そんな贅沢をするかと人が問うと、石鹸は石鹸でなくてはいけない。偽物を使う位なら使わないと言っている。五分刈頭を洗う。それから裸になって体じゅうを丁寧に拭く。同じ金だらいで下湯を使う。足を洗う。人が汚いと言うと、己の体は清潔だと言っている。湯をバケツに棄てる。水をその跡に取って手拭を洗う。水を棄てる。手拭を絞って金だらいを拭く。又手拭を絞って掛ける。一日に二度づつこれだけの事をする。湯屋には行かない。その代わり戦地でも舎営をしている間は、これだけのことを廃せないのである。

　石田は襦袢袴下を着替えて又夏衣袴を着た。常の日は、

presents, he had them all returned. The old woman had already observed this much about him.

When she stood up to leave the room, Ishida asked, "Is the hot water ready?"

"Yes, sir," she said, and withdrew to the kitchen.

Ishida went to the corner-room at the rear of the house. Here there were set out a water pitcher, a bowl for gargling, a metal basin with hot water, and a bucket. This arrangement was decided on from the first day; the routine was always the same, morning and evening.

First Ishida brushed his teeth. Then he gargled. Then he washed his face with hot water. (The soap he used was an import costing about 70 sen. When anyone asked him why he went to such an extravagance, he would say, "Soap has to be real soap; if I have to use a poor imitation I might as well use none at all.") Then he washed his short-cropped head. Next he took off his clothes and carefully wiped himself all over. He used the same water basin for a hip bath. And finally, he washed his feet. (To those who said it was unhygienic his answer always was: "My body is clean.") The hot water he emptied into the bucket. Then he poured cold water into the basin and washed the hand towel. He emptied the cold water. Next he squeezed out the hand towel and wiped the water basin. He squeezed out the hand towel again and draped it over the basin. Twice a day he went through this whole routine. He never went to the public bathhouse. One advantage, however, was that, even on the battlefield, as long as he was billeted he could maintain this much of a routine at least.

Ishida changed into fresh undershirt and undershorts and then put on his summer uniform again. On

寝巻に浴衣を着るまで、このままでいる。それを客が来て見て、「野木さんの流儀か」と言うと、「野木閣下の事は知らない」と言うのである。

机の前に座る。膳がでる。どんなにゆっくり食っても、十五分より長く掛かったことはない。

外を見れば雨が止んでいる。石田は起って台所に出た。飯を食っている婆さんが箸を置くのを見て「用ではない」と言いながら、土間に降りる縁に出た。土間には虎吉が鳥に米を蒔いて遣って、しゃがんで見ている。石田も鳥を見に出たのである。

大きな雄鶏である。総身の羽が赤褐色で、頭に柑子色の領巻があって、黒い尾を長く垂れている。

虎吉は人の悪そうな青黒い顔をあげて、ぎょろりとした目で主人を見て、こう言った。

「旦那。こいつは肉が軟ですぜ。」

「食うのではない。」

「へえ。飼って置くのですか。」

「うむ。」

「そんなら、大家さんの物置に伏籠の明いているのがあったから、あれを借りて来ましょう。」

「買うまでは借りても好い。」

40

a normal day he would stay this way until he put on the light kimono he wore for sleeping. If a visitor, seeing him dressed this way, said, "Following Lord Nogi's example, eh?" he would say, "I know nothing about His Excellency Lord Nogi."

He sat in front of his desk. His meal was then brought to him. No matter how leisurely he ate, it never took him longer than fifteen minutes.

He looked outside. The rain had stopped. He stood up and went into the kitchen. The old woman was eating. When he noticed her put her chopsticks down, he said, "It's all right," and he went out to the floored area whence one descended to the earthen floor. Torakichi was down in the earth-floor area, hunkered down and watching the chicken eat the rice he was throwing it. Ishida had also come to see the chicken.

It was a large rooster. It had reddish-brown feathers all over its body, with an orange collar around its neck, and a long, drooping, black tail.

Torakichi lifted his ill-natured looking, bluish-black face and looked at Ishida with his goggly eyes. "Master," he said, "the meat on this thing is tender."

"It's not for eating."

"Huh!? You're going to keep it?"

"Yes."

"In that case, there's a big hamper in the landlord's storage shed that's not being used. I'll go and borrow it."

"You can borrow it until we buy one."

　こういって置いて、石田は居間に帰って、刀を弔って、帽を被って玄関に出た。玄関には島村が磨いて置いた長靴がある。それを庭におろしてはく。がたがたいう音を聞き附けて婆さんが出て来た。

「お外套は。」

「すぐ帰るから入らん。」

　石田は鍛治町を西へ真っ直ぐに鳥町まで出た。そこにこないだ名刺を置いて歩いたとき見て置いた鳥屋がある。そこで牝鶏を一羽買って、伏籠を職人に注文して貰うように頼んだ。鳥は羽の色の真っ白な、むくむくと太ったのを見立てて買った。跡から持たせておこすということである。石田は代を払って帰った。

　牝鶏を持って来た。虎吉は鳥屋をうまやの方へ連れて行って何か話し込んでいる。石田は雌雄を一しょに放して、雄鶏が片々の羽をひろげて、雌のまわりを半圏状に歩いて挑むのを見ている。雌は兎角逃げよう逃げようとしているのである。

　間もなく、まだ外は明るいのに、鳥は不安の様子をして来た。その内、台所の土間の隅に棚のあるのを見附けて、それへ飛び上がろうとする。ねぐらを捜すのである。石田は別当に、「鳥を寝かすようにして遣れ」と言って居

Having said this, Ishida returned to the sitting room, strapped on his sabre, put his cap on, and went to the front entrance. There, polished and shined by Shimamura, were his boots. He set them down on the ground and stepped into them. The old woman heard the clatter and came to the front door.

"Your coat, sir?"

"I don't need it. I won't be long."

Ishida went due west down Kaji-machi till he came to Tori-machi. There was a poultry shop there that he had seen recently when walking around leaving his name cards. He bought a hen at the shop and requested that an order be given to the craftsman for a large hamper. The hen he selected was a plump one with pure white feathers. He would have it delivered afterwards, the man said. Ishida paid and went home.

The hen was delivered. Torakichi took the poultry man towards the stable and had a long conversation with him. Ishida set the rooster and the hen loose together and watched the rooster spread now one wing now the other and make advances to the hen in a semi-circular strut around her. The hen, meantime, kept trying to run away.

In a short while, even though it was still light out, the birds began to act troubled. Then they caught sight of a shelf in one corner of the earth-floor area in the kitchen, and they tried to fly up to it. They were looking for a place to roost. "Fix it so the birds can roost there," Ishida said to the stableman, and then went back to the

間に入った。

　翌日からは夜明けに鶏が鳴く。石田は愉快だと思った。ところが午後引けて帰って見ると、牝鶏が二羽になっている。婆さんに問えば別当が自分のを一羽一しょに飼わせて貰いたいと言ったということである。石田は嫌な顔をしたが、咎めもしなかった。二三日立つうちに、又牝鶏が一羽殖えて雄鶏共に四羽になった。今度のも別当ので、どこかから貰って来たのだということであった。石田は又嫌な顔をしたが、やはり別当には何とも言わなかった。

　四羽の鶏が屋敷中をあさって歩く。薄井の方の茄子畑に侵入して、爺さんに追われて帰ることもある。牝鶏同志で喧嘩をするので、別当が強い奴を捕まえて伏篭に伏せて置く。伏篭はもう出来て来た新しいので、隣から借りた分は返してしまったのである。鳥屋は別当が薄井の爺さんにことわって、縁の下を仕切ってこしらえて、入口には板切と割竹と互違に打ち附けた不細工な格子戸をはめた。

　ある日婆さんが、石田の司令部から帰るのを待ち受けて、こう言った。

　「別当さんの鳥が玉子を生んだそうで、旦那様が上がる

sitting room.

The next morning the rooster crowed at daybreak. Ishida was delighted. When he quit work in the afternoon and returned home, however, there were *two* hens. He asked the old woman about it, and she told him that the stableman had said he wished to be allowed to raise his chicken with the others. A look of displeasure passed over Ishida's face, but he didn't say anything against it. A few days later another hen appeared, so that now there were four chickens, including the rooster. This one was also the stableman's, he had received it from somebody, the old woman said. Again a look of displeasure passed over Ishida's face, but again he said nothing to the stableman.

The four chickens went round scratching up the whole property. At times they invaded the landlord's eggplant patch and were chased out by the old man. The hens fought among themselves, so the stableman caught the strongest one and confined it under the hamper. This was the new hamper, already finished; the one borrowed from the landlord had been returned. After discussing the matter beforehand with the landlord, the stableman made a coop by partitioning off a section under the verandah; across the opening he fitted a clumsy lattice-work door made by nailing strips of wood alternately with split bamboo.

One day the old woman was waiting for Ishida when he returned. "The stableman says his chickens have laid some eggs," she said, "and that if you'll eat

なら上げてくれと言いなさりますが。」

「入らんと言え。」

　婆さんは驚いたような顔をして引き下がった。これか
らは婆さんが度々卵の話をする。どうも別当の牝鶏に
限って卵を生んで、旦那様のは生まないという。婆さん
はこの話をする度に、極めて声を小さくする。そして不
思議だ不思議だという。婆さんはこの話の裏面に、別に
何物かがあるのを石田に発見して貰いたいのである。と
ころが石田にはどうしてもそれが分からないらしい。ど
うも馬鹿なのだから、分からないでも仕ようがない。そ
こでじれったがりながら、反復して同じ事を言う。しか
し自分の言うことが別当に聞こえるのはこわいので、次
第に声は小さくなるのである。とうとうしまいには石田
の耳の根に摩り寄って、こう言った。

「こねえな事を言うては悪うござりまするが、玉子は旦
那様の鳥も生まんことはござりません。どれが生んでも、
別当さんが自分の鳥が生んだというのでござりますが
な。」

　婆さんはおそるおそるこう言って、石田が怒って大声
を出さねば好いがと思っていた。ところが石田は少しも
感動しない。平気な顔をしている。婆さんはじれったく

46

them, I should fix them for you."

"Tell him I don't want any."

With a look of great surprise, the old woman turned and left. But later on the old woman brought up the topic of eggs several times. "Strange," she would say, "but only the stableman's hens are laying eggs and Master's isn't." Whenever she mentioned the subject she would speak in a very low voice. "Strange, very strange," she would say. She was trying to get Ishida to catch on that there was more behind what she was saying. But Ishida just didn't seem to catch on at all. "Big fool that he is, if he don't know what's up what's the use?" she thought. Then, impatiently, she brought the same thing up all over again. But because she was afraid the stableman might hear what she was saying, her voice gradually got lower and lower. Finally, she ended up leaning close to Ishida's ear and whispering,

"It's wrong of me to say a thing like this, but it isn't true that Master's hen isn't laying eggs. No matter which hen lays the eggs, the stableman says it was his hen that laid them."

The old woman spoke nervously. She was afraid Ishida would get angry and raise his voice. But Ishida didn't react in the slightest. The expression on his face was one of unconcern. The old woman was fit to be tied.

て溜まらない。今度は別当に知れても好いから怒って貰いたいような気がする。そしてとうとう馬鹿に附ける薬はないとあきらめた。

石田は暫く黙っていて、極めて冷然としてこう言った。

「己は玉子が食いたいときには買うて食う。」

婆さんは歯痒いのを我慢するという風で、何か口の内でぶつぶつ言いながら、勝手へ下がった。

七月十日は石田が小倉へ来てからの三度目の日曜日であった。石田は早く起きて、例の狭い間で手水を使った。これまでは日曜日にも用事があったが、今日は始めて日曜日らしく感じた。寝巻の浴衣を着たままで、兵児帯をぐるぐると巻いて、南側の裏縁に出た。南国の空は紺青色に晴れていて、蜜柑の茂みを洩れる日が、きらきらした斑紋を、花壇の周囲の砂の上に印している。厩には馬の手入れをする金櫛の音がしている。折々馬が足を踏み更えるので、蹄鉄が厩の敷板に触れてことことという。そうすると別当が「こら」と言って馬を叱っている。石田は気がのんびりするような心持ちで、朝の空気を深く呼吸した。

石田は、縁の隅に新聞反古の上に、裏と裏とを合わせて上げてあった麻裏を取って、庭に卸して、縁から降り

She didn't care any more if the stableman heard or not, she wanted Ishida to get angry. But then she finally concluded there was no curing a fool, and she gave up.

Ishida sat silent for a time, then in an exceedingly calm voice said, "When I want to eat eggs I'll buy some."

Suppressing her rage, but muttering under her breath, the old woman retired to the kitchen.

The tenth of July was the third Sunday after Ishida's arrival in Kokura. He rose early and washed himself in the small room as usual. Till now he had had business to attend to even on Sundays, and this was the first time a Sunday felt like a Sunday to him. Still in his sleeping kimono, he tightened the plain sash and went out to the rear verandah on the south side of the house. The Kyushu sky was a clear deep blue, and the sun coming through the foliage of the mandarin trees made bright spots on the sand around the flower bed. From the stable came the sound of the metal comb being used to groom the horse. Now and then the horse would shift position, and the horseshoes would go clop, clop, on the stable floorboards. Every time the horse moved like this the stableman would yell "Hey!" at it. With a feeling of great tranquillity, Ishida took deep breaths of the morning air.

He picked up a pair of hemp-soled straw sandals left, sole-to-sole, atop a pile of old newspapers, set them down on the ground, and stepped into them from the

立った。

花壇のまわりをぶらぶら歩く。庭の井戸の石畳にいつもの赤い蟹のいるのを見て、井戸を上から覗くと、蟹は皆隠れてしまう。苔の附いた弔瓶に短い竿を附けたのが放り込んである。弔瓶と石畳との間を忙しげに水馬が走っている。

一本の蜜柑の木を東へ回ると勝手口に出る。婆さんが味噌汁を煮ている。別当は馬の手入れをしまって、蹄に油を塗って、勝手口に来た。手には飼桶を持っている。主人に会釈をして、勝手口に置いてある麦箱の蓋を開けて、麦を飼桶に入れている。石田は暫く立って見ている。

「いくら食うか。」

「ええ。これで三杯ぐらいが丁度宜しいので。」

別当はぎょろっとした目で、横に主人を見て、麦箱の中に放り込んである、縁の欠けた轆轤細工の飯鉢を取って見せる。石田は黙って背中を向けて、縁側の方へ引き返した。

花壇の所まで帰った頃に、牝鶏が一羽けたたましい鳴声をして足元に駆けて来た。それと一しょに妙な声が聞こえた。丸で蛞々児の鳴くようにやかましい女の声である。石田が声の方角を見ると、花壇の向こうの畠を仕切っ

verandah.

He set out for a leisurely walk around the flower bed. Noticing the ever-present red crabs in the rock crevices in the garden well, he peered down the well. The crabs all hid from view. A moss-covered water bucket with a short pole attached to it had been left in the well. A water spider busily raced up and back between the water bucket and the rock wall of the well.

Past a mandarin tree he turned toward the east and ended up by the back door. The old woman was boiling *miso* soup. The stableman, having finished grooming the horse and putting oil on its hooves, came to the back door. He was carrying a feed pail. Making a bow to Ishida, he removed the lid of the oat bin beside the back door and started filling the pail with oats. For a while Ishida stood and watched.

"How much does it eat?"

"Oh, three of these will be about enough." Looking sideways at his master with those goggle eyes of his, he showed Ishida a lathe-turned, wooden feeding bowl, part of its rim missing, that he picked up from inside the oat bin. Ishida turned around without a word and returned in the direction of the verandah.

He had come as far as the flower bed when a hen came running up to him, squawking loudly. At the same time he heard a peculiar voice. It was a woman's voice, strident as a noisy cricket. Turning in the direction of the voice, he saw, looking over the hedge fence

た、南隣の生垣の上から顔を出している四十位の女がいる。下太りのかぼちゃのように黄いろい顔で頭のてっぺんには、油固めの小さい丸髷が載っている。これが声の主である。

何か盛んにしゃべっている。石田は誰に言っているかと思って、自分の周囲を見廻したが、別に誰もいない。石田の感ずる所では、自分に言っているとは思われない。しかし自分に聞かせる為に言っているらしい。日曜日で自分の内にいるのを候っていてしゃべり出したかと思われる。謂わば天下に呼号して、旁ら石田をして聞かしめんとするのである。

言うことが好くは分からない。一体この土地には限らず、方言というものは、怒って悪口を言うような時、最も純粋に現われるものである。目上の人に物を言ったり何かすることになれば、修飾するから特色がなくなってしまう。この女の今しゃべっているのが、純粋な豊前語である。

そこで内のお時婆さんや家主の爺さんの話と違って、おおよその意味は聞き取れるが、細かいnuancesは聞き取れない。何でも鶏が垣を越えて行って畠を荒らして困るということらしい。それを主題にして堂々たる

separating the vegetable patch beyond the flower bed from the property of the neighbor to the south, a woman of about forty. She had a face like a yellow pumpkin, and on the very peak of her head lay a round chignon, plastered down with hair oil. She was the owner of the voice.

She was talking at a furious rate. Ishida looked around to see whom she was talking to, but there was nobody there besides him. He had the impression that she was not talking to him, and yet it seemed she was saying it for him to hear. He couldn't help feeling that she must have been waiting for him to be at home on a Sunday and then had launched into a tirade. Shouting from the rooftops, as it were, she wanted to make sure Ishida got the message as well.

He wasn't quite sure what it was she was saying. It wasn't true only of this region, dialects everywhere tend to appear in their purest forms at times such as this, when someone is angrily complaining about something. When one is talking to a superior one embellishes one's speech, thus doing away with all individuality. It was pure Buzen dialect that this woman was speaking at the moment.

As a result, in contrast to the speech of the old woman Toki and that of his landlord, he was able to grasp the general tenor of her words but missed all the fine nuances. At any rate, she seemed to be saying that the chickens were crossing the fence and tearing up her vegetable garden. That was the main theme of the

Philippicaを発しているのである。女はこんな事を言う。豊前には諺がある。何 町歩とかの畑を持たないでは、鶏を飼ってはならないというのである。然るに借家ずまいをしていて鶏を飼うなんぞというのは僭越も亦 甚しい。サアベルをさして馬に騎っているものは何をしても好いと思うのは心得違である。

大抵こんな筋であって、攻撃余力を残さない。女はこんな事も言う。鶏が何をしているか知らないばかりではない。雇い婆さんが勝手の物をごまかして、自分の内の暮らしを立てているのも知るまい。別当が馬の麦をごまかして金を溜めようとしているのも知るまい。こういうときは声を一層張り上げる。婆さんにも別当にも聞かせようとするのである。

女はこんな事も言う。借家人のすることは家主の責任である。サアベルがこわくて物が言えないようなら、サアベルなんぞに始めから家を貸さないが好い。声はいよいよ高くなる。薄井の爺さんにも聞かせようとするのである。

石田は花壇の前に棒のように立って、しゃべる女の方へ真向に向いて、黙って聞いている。顔にはおりおり微笑の影が、風の無い日に木葉が揺らぐように動く外には、

54

mighty philippic she was delivering. She had the following to say as well: There was a common saying in Buzen that if you didn't have so and so many square meters of land you shouldn't raise chickens. But to be living in a rented house and to raise chickens was the height of presumptuousness. Anyone who thinks he can do what he pleases because he wears a sabre and rides a horse is badly mistaken.

This was the general drift of her words, spoken with no letup in her verbal barrage. She had the following to say as well: He not only doesn't know what his chickens are doing, he also doesn't even know that the old woman he hired was cheating on things in the kitchen and keeping her own family alive on the things she took. He doesn't even know that the stableman is cheating on the amount of oats in order to save on his own money. For these last two items her voice rose in intensity. She wanted to be sure the old woman and the stableman heard, too.

She had more to say: What someone renting a house did was the responsibility of the owner of the house. If he was so afraid of a sabre that he couldn't say anything then he shouldn't have leased the house to someone with a sabre in the first place. Her voice had risen higher and higher. She wanted old Usui to hear, too.

Ishida stood straight as a ramrod in front of the flower bed, facing directly at the speaker, and listened without a word. Except for an occasional smile that flickered across his lips, much as the leaves on a tree might stir from time to time even on a windless day,

何の表情もない。軍服を来て上官の小言を聞いている時と大抵同じ事ではあるが、少し筋肉が弛んでいるだけ違う。微笑の浮かぶのを制せないだけ違う。

石田はこんな事を思っている。鶏は垣を越すものと見える。坊主が酒を般若湯ということは世間に流布しているが、鶏を鑽籬菜というということは本を読まないものは知らない。鶏を貰った所が、食いたくもなかったので、生かして置こうと思った。生かして置けば垣も越す。垣を越すかも知れないということまで、初めに考えなかったのは、用意が足りないようではあるが、何をするにもそんなéventualitéを眼中に置いては出来ようがない。鶏を飼うという事実に、この女が怒るという事実が付帯して来るのは、格別驚くべきわけでもない。なんにしろ、あの垣の上に妙な首が載っていて、その首が何の遠慮もなく表情筋を伸縮させて、雄弁を揮っている所は面白い。東京にいたとき、光線の反射を利用して、卓の上に載せた首が物を言うように思わせる見世物を見たことがあった。あれは見世物師が余りprétentieuxであったので、こっちの反感を起こして面白くなかった。あれよりはこの方が余程面白い。石田はこんな事を思っている。

56

his face was expressionless. It was almost like being in uniform and being lectured to by a superior officer, except that his muscles were slightly less tense, and that he did not suppress the occasional flicker of a smile.

This is what ran through his mind: It seems chickens by their nature cross hedges. It was common knowledge that Buddhist monks refer to sake as "wisdom brew," but unless you read books you wouldn't know that they also refer to chickens as "fence-crossing vegetables."* He had received a rooster, but since he hadn't wanted to eat it he had decided to let it live. Once you let it live it'll get through hedges. It seemed as if he lacked foresight, not considering from the start the possibility it might go through fences; but it wasn't possible to visualize such eventualities in everything you did. There was no particular cause to get excited if the fact of his raising chickens was followed incidentally by the fact of this woman being angry. At any rate, the way that extraordinary head was suspended above the fence, without the slightest reserve expanding and contracting its facial muscles in the exercise of oratorical power, was amusing. When he was in Tokyo he had seen a show in which reflections of light rays were used to make the audience think a head lying on a table top was speaking. That time, though, the pretentiousness of the showman had aroused his antipathy, and he hadn't found it amusing at all. This performance was much more entertaining than that one. These were the sort of things going through Ishida's mind.

* By using these names, the monks justified drinking sake and eating meat.

垣の上の女は雄弁家ではある。しかしいかなる雄弁家も一の論題に就いてしゃべり得る論旨には限りがある。垣の上の女もとうとう思想が涸渇した。察するに、彼は思想の涸渇を感じると共に失望の念を作すことを禁じ得なかったのであろう。彼は経験上こんな雄弁を弄する度に、誰か相手になってくれる。少なくとも一言くらい何とか言ってくれる。そうすれば、水の流れが石に触れて激するように、弁論に張合が出て来る。相手も雄弁を弄することになれば、旗鼓相当って、彼の心が飽き足るであろう。彼は石田のような相手には始めて出逢ったであろう。そして暖簾に腕押しをしたような不愉快な感じをしたであろう。彼は「ええとも、今度来たら締めてしまうから」と言い放って、境の生垣の蔭へ南瓜に似た首を引込めた。結末は意味の振っている割に、声に力がなかった。

「旦那さん。御膳が出来ましたが。」

婆さんに呼ばれて、石田は朝飯を食いに座敷へ戻った。給仕をしながら婆さんが、南裏の上さんは評判の悪者で、誰も相手にならないのだというような意味の事を話した。石田はなるたけ鳥を伏篭に伏せて置くようにしろと言い付けた。そのとき婆さんは声を低うしてこういう

The woman hovering over the hedge was an eloquent orator. But there are only so many points even an eloquent orator can make on any one theme. Eventually ideas ran dry for the woman at the hedge, too. It seemed to Ishida that as she felt her ideas drying up, she couldn't suppress a feeling of disappointment. In past experience, every time she brought such eloquence into play, it had always produced a reaction from somebody, even if only a word or two. In that event, the argument would take on new force, just as the flow of water speeds up when it comes in contact with a rock. If that other person were also to bring some eloquence into play, the lists would be entered with colors flying and drums playing, and her heart's desires would be fulfilled. She probably had never met anyone like Ishida. It must have been like the awkward feeling of trying to lean against a curtain.

"Very well, next time one comes I'm going to wring its neck, you'll see!"

With this parting salvo, she pulled in her pumpkin-like head and disappeared on the other side of the hedge dividing the two properties. In her *dénouement*, her voice had lacked a conviction commensurate with the threat expressed.

"Master, your meal is ready."

At the old woman's call, Ishida went back to the sitting room to eat breakfast. As she served him, she told him, in so many words, that the lady on the south side had a reputation for being a disagreeable person and nobody had anything to do with her. Ishida ordered her to keep the chickens confined under their hampers as far as possible. At this, the old woman lowered her

ことを言った。主人の買って来た、白い牝鶏が今朝は卵を抱いている。別当も白い牝鶏の抱いているのを、他の牝鶏が生んだとは言いにくいと見えて黙っている。卵をたった一つ孵させるのは無駄だから、取って来ようかと言うのである。石田は、「抱いているなら構わずに抱かせて置け。」と言った。

　石田は飯を済ませてから、勝手へ出て見た。まだ縁の下の鳥屋の出来ない内に寝かしたことのある、台所の土間の上の棚がわらを敷いたままになっていた。白い牝鶏はその上に上がっている。常からむくむくした鳥であるのが、羽を立てて体をふくらまして、いつもの二倍位の大きさになって、首だけ動かしてあちこちを見ている。茶碗を洗っていた婆さんが来て鳥の横腹をつつく。鳥は声を立てる。石田は婆さんの方を見て言った。

「どうするのだ。」

「旦那さんに玉子を見せて上げようと思いまして。」

「よせ。見せんでもいい。」

　石田は思い出したように、婆さんにこう言うことを問うた。世帯を持つとき、桝を買った筈だが、別当はあれで麦を量りはしないかと言うのである。婆さんは、別当の桝を使ったのは見たことがないと言った。石田は「そ

voice and said: "The white hen that Master bought is sitting on an egg this morning. The stableman isn't saying anything; seems even he can't say the egg the white hen is sitting on was laid by one of the other hens. It's not much use to let only a single egg hatch; shall I go and collect it?"

"If it's sitting on it don't bother it, let it sit on it!" Ishida said.

After he finished eating, he went to the kitchen area to have a look. Straw was still strewn atop the shelf in the earth-floor part of the kitchen where they had let the chickens roost before the coop was built under the verandah. The white hen was on this shelf. A plump bird to begin with, now, with its feathers ruffled to fluff out its body, it was about twice its usual size, and only its head moved as it looked this way and that. The old woman stopped in the middle of washing dishes and came over and poked the hen in the side. The bird let out a squawk. Ishida looked at the old woman and said, "What did you do that for?"

"I thought I would let Master see the egg."

"Never mind. You don't have to show me."

As if he just remembered something, Ishida then asked the old woman a question: "When I moved in, I thought sure I bought a measuring box; wasn't the stableman measuring the oats with that box?" The old woman said that she had never seen the stableman using a measuring box. "Oh?" he said, and straightaway

うか」といって、ついと部屋に帰った。そして将校行李の蓋を開けて、半切毛布に包んだ箱を出した。Havanaの葉巻である。石田は平生天狗を呑んでいて、これならどんな田舎に行軍をしても、補充の出来ない事はないと言っている。たまには上等の葉巻を呑む。そして友達と雑談をするとき、「小説家なんぞは物を知らない、金剛石入の指輪を嵌めた金持の主人公にManilaを呑ませる」なぞと言って笑うのである。石田がたまに呑む葉巻を毛布にくるんで置くのは、火薬の保存法を応用しているのである。石田はこう言っている。己だって大将にでもなれば、煙草も毎日新しい箱を開けるのだ。今のうちは箱を開けてから一月も保存しなくてはならないのだから、工夫を要すると言っている。

石田は葉巻に火を付けて、さも愉快げに、一吸吸って、例の手習机に向かった。北向きの表庭は、百日紅の疎な葉越しに、日が一ぱいにさして、夾竹桃にはもうところどころ花が咲いている。向かいの内の糸車は、今日もぶうんぶうんと鳴っている。

石田は床の間の隅に立て掛けてある洋書の中からLa Bruyère の性格という本を抽き出して、短い鋭い章を一つ読んではじっと考えて見る。*又一つ読んではじっと考

he returned to his room. There he opened the lid of his officer's traveling case and took out a box wrapped in a half-blanket. It was a box of Havana cigars. Ordinarily he smoked Japanese cigars; no matter how remote the countryside they might march to, he would always be able to replenish these, he used to say. Occasionally, however, he would smoke a high-class cigar. When chatting with friends he used to laugh and say, "Novelists are ignoramuses. They have their wealthy heroes wear rings studded with diamonds, then have them smoking Manilas." By rolling up in a blanket the cigars that he smoked only occasionally, Ishida was making applied use of a method of preserving gunpowder. He used to explain: "If I ever get to be a general, I'll open a new box of cigars every day. For the time being I have to preserve them a whole month after I open the box, so it takes some ingenuity."

Ishida lit his cigar, took a puff, and sat in front of the familiar student desk. In the front garden with its northern exposure, the sun was beating full down over the patches of crepe myrtle leaves, and flowers were already blooming here and there on the sweet oleanders. The spinning wheel across the street was humming its tune, even on a Sunday.

From among the Western books lined up against one corner of the tokonoma, Ishida picked out La Bruyère's *Les Caractères*. He read one of the short, incisive sections and reflected on it quietly. He read an-

---

* Jean de La Bruyère (1645–1696) is known for this one work, which is a collection of satirical sketches of different types of people, and different kinds of behavior, current in France at his time.

えて見る。五六章も読んだかと思うと本を措いた。

　それから舶来の象牙紙と封筒との箱入になっているのを出して、ペンで手紙を書き出した。石田はペンと鉛筆とで万事済ませて、硯というものを使わない。稀に願届けなどが入れば、書記に頼む。それは陸軍に出てから病気引き籠りをしたことがないという位だから、めったに入らない。

　人から来た手紙で、返事をしなくてはならないのは、図嚢の中に入れているのだから、それを出して片端から返事を書くのである。東京に、中学に入っている息子を母に附けて置いてある。第一に母に遣る手紙を書いた。それから筆を措かずに二つ三つ書いた。そして母の手紙だけを将校行李にしまって、外の手紙は引き裂いてしまった。

　午になった。飯を済ませて、さっきの手紙を書き始めるとき、灰皿の上に置いた葉巻の呑みさしに火を附けて、北表の縁に出た。空はいつの間にか薄い灰色になっている。汽車の音がする。

　「蝙蝠傘張り替え修繕は好うがすの」と呼んで、前の往来を通るものがある。糸車のぶうんぶんは相変らず根調をなしている。

other one and reflected on it quietly. After reading maybe five or six sections, he put the book down.

Next, he took some imported ivory-paper and envelopes from a box and started writing a letter, using a pen. Ishida always made do with a pen and pencil; he never used an inkstone and brush. When on rare occasions he needed to present a formal request for something, he would ask a secretary to do it. Since he had almost never been laid up by sickness since joining the army, he rarely needed such services.

Personal letters that had to be answered he kept inside the officer's pouch he always wore strapped to his belt; these he would take out and write answers to in one sitting. He had a son in Tokyo, going to junior high school, whom he had left with his own mother. First of all he wrote a letter to his mother. Afterwards, without stopping, he wrote a few more. His mother's own letter he put inside his officer's traveling case, the others' letters he tore up.

It was lunchtime. After finishing his meal, he lit the cigar butt he had left on the ashtray earlier, when he began writing letters, and went out onto the front verandah. A light gray had stolen over the sky. He heard the sound of a train.

"Umbrellas re-covered and repaired . . ." cried someone walking down the street. The humming of the spinning wheel provided the basic rhythm as usual.

石田はどこか出ようかと思ったが、空模様が変わっているので、止める気になった。暫くして座敷へ入って、南アフリカの大きい地図をひろげて、その頃戦争が起こりそうになっているTransvaalの地理を調べている。こんな風で一日は暮れた。

三四日立ってからの事である。もう役所は午引けになっている。石田は馬に蹄鉄を打たせに遣ったので、司令部から引き掛けに、紫川の左岸の狭い道を常磐橋の方へ歩いていると、戦役以来心安くしていた中野という男に逢った。中野の方から声を掛ける。

「おい。今日は徒歩かい。」

「うむ。鉄を打ちに遣ったのだ。君はどうしたのだ。」

「僕のは海に入れに遣った。」

「そうかい。」

「非常に喜ぶぜ。」

「そんなら僕も一遍遣って見よう。」

「別当が泳げなくちゃあだめだ。」

「泳げるようなことを言っていた。」

中野は石田より早く卒業した士官である。今は石田と同じ歩兵少佐で、大隊長をしている。少し太り過ぎている男で、性質から言えば老実家である。馬をひどく可哀

66

Ishida had intended to go out for a walk somewhere, but with the change in the cast of the sky he no longer felt like going out. After a few minutes he went to the sitting room; spreading out a large map of southern Africa, he studied the geography of Transvaal, where an outbreak of war seemed imminent. In this fashion, the day drew to a close.

Several days passed. By this time he was already finishing work at the office by noon. On this particular day Ishida had sent his horse to be shoed, and he was walking back from headquarters along the narrow road on the left bank of Murasaki River, headed towards Tokiwa Bridge, when he met up with a good friend from the Russian War days, Nakano by name. It was Nakano who called out first.

"Hey! Footin' it today, eh?"

"Yes. I sent it to get shoed. What've you done with yours?"

"I let it be taken for a dip in the ocean."

"Oh?"

"It loves it."

"I'll have to try that, too, then."

"Your stableman has to be able to swim."

"He said something about being able to swim."

Nakano had graduated from the officers school earlier than Ishida. At present he was a major in the infantry, same as Ishida, and a battalion commander. Slightly overweight, temperamentally he was a hardworking type. He bestowed extreme care on his horse.

がる。中野は話を続けた。

「君に逢ったら、いつか言って置こうと思ったが、ここには大きな溝に石を並べて蓋をした所があるがなあ。」

「あの馬借に往く通りだろう。」

「あれだ。魚町だ。あの上を馬で歩いちゃあいかんぜ。馬は人間とは目方が違うからなあ。」

「うむ。そうかも知れない。ちっとも気が付かなかった。」

こんな話をして常磐橋に掛かった。中野が何か思い出したという様子で、歩度を緩めてこう言った。

「おう。それからも一つ君に話して置きたいことがあった。馬鹿な事だがなあ。」

「何だい。僕はまだ来たばかりで、なんにも知らないんだから、どしどし注意を与えてくれ給え。」

「実は僕の内の縁がわからは、君の内の門が見えるので、妻の奴が妙な事を発見したというのだ。」

「はてな。」

「君が毎日出勤すると、あの門から婆さんが風呂敷包を持って出て行くというのだ。ところが一昨日だったかと思う、その包が非常に大きいというので、妻がひどく心配していたよ。」

「そうか。そう言われれば心当がある。いつも漬物を切

Nakano went on. "There was something I meant to tell you about the next time we met. There's a place here where they've covered over a ditch with a row of flat stones."

"You mean on the road going to Bashaku?"

"That's it. In Uo-machi. You mustn't ride your horse over that. Horses don't weigh the same as people, you know."

"Hmm, I guess you're right. I hadn't given it much thought."

At this point in the conversation they had arrived at Tokiwa Bridge. Nakano seemed to remember something, and, slackening his pace, he said, "Say, there was one more thing I wanted to talk to you about. It's a silly thing, but. . . ."

"What is it? I've practically just arrived here and don't know a thing, so, please, feel free to give me as much advice as you can.

"To tell the truth, the front gate of your place can be seen from the verandah of my place, and my wife says she's noticed something strange."

"My word!"

"She says that, every day after you've left for work, the old woman goes out by that gate with a *furoshiki* bundle in her hand. But two days ago, I believe it was, the bundle was huge, my wife said. She was terribly concerned."

"I see. Now that you mention it, I think I know what it was. We're always running out of pickled vege-

らすので、あの日には茄子と胡瓜を沢山に漬けて置けと言ったのだ。」

「それじゃあ自分の内へも沢山漬けたのだろう。」

「はははは。しかし兎に角有難う。奥さんにも宜しく言ってくれ給え。」

　話しながら京町の入口まで来たが、石田は立ち留まった。

「僕は寄って行く所があった。ここで失敬する。」

「そうか。さようなら。」

　石田は常磐橋を渡って跡へ戻った。そして室町の達見へ寄って、お上さんに下女を取り替えることを頼んだ。お上さんは狆の頭をさすりながら、笑ってこう言った。

「あんた様は婆さんがええとお言いなされたがな。」

「婆さんはいかん。」

「何かしましたかな。」

「何もしたのじゃない。大分えらそうだから、丈夫な若いのをよこすように、口入れの方へ頼んで下さい。」

「はいはい。別品さんを上げるように言うて遣ります。」

「いや。下女に別品は困る。さようなら。」

　石田はそれから帰り掛けに隣へ寄って、薄井の爺さんに、下女の若いのが来るから、どうぞお前さんの所の下

tables, so that morning I had told her to pickle plenty of eggplant and cucumbers."

"So she must've pickled plenty for her own family, too."

"Ha ha ha ha! But anyway, thanks for telling me. And convey my regards to your wife."

While talking they had come to the street leading to Kyō-machi. There Ishida came to a halt.

"There was a place I was to drop in on the way. I'll have to excuse myself here."

"Sure. Be seein' you."

Ishida recrossed Tokiwa Bridge and went back part of the way he'd come. He called at the "Tatsumi" in Muro-machi and asked the landlady to arrange a change in housemaids. Stroking her lapdog's head, the landlady laughed and said, "You said you wanted an old woman, right?"

"An old woman won't do."

"Has she done something wrong?"

"It's not because she's done something wrong. It seems to be too hard on her, so please ask the employment woman to send a young, strong one."

"Yes, as you wish. I'll tell her to give you a pretty girl."

"No, I don't want a pretty girl for a housemaid. Good-bye now."

Before returning to his house Ishida stopped at his landlord's house next door and asked old Usui if he would let his housemaid come to stay the nights at his

女を夜だけ泊まりに来させて下さいと頼んだ。そして内へ帰って黙っていた。

翌日口入れの上さんが来て、お時婆さんに話をした。年寄に骨を折らせるのが気の毒だと、旦那が言うからと言ったそうである。婆さんは存外素直に聞いて帰ることになった。石田はまだ月の半ばであるのに、一箇月分の給料を遣った。

夕方になって、口入れの上さんは出直して、目見えの女中を連れて来た。二十五六位の髪の薄い女で、お辞儀をしながら、横目で石田の顔を見る。襦袢の袖にしている水浅葱のめりんすが、一寸位、袖口から覗いている。

石田は翌日島村を口入れ屋へ遣って、下女を取り替えることを言い付けさせた。今度は十六ばかりの小柄で目のくりくりしたのが来た。気性もはきはきしているらしい。これが石田の気に入った。

二三日置いて見て、石田はこれに決めた。比那古のもので、春というのだそうだ。男のような肥後詞を使って、動作も活発である。肌に琥珀色の澤があって、筋肉が締まっている。石田は精悍な奴だと思った。

しかし困ることには、いつも茶の竪縞の単物を着ているが、膝の所には二所ばかりつぎが当っている。それで

place since he was getting a young housemaid. Then he went home and said nothing.

The following day, the employment woman came and had a talk with the old woman, Toki. She told her the master said he felt sorry about making an elderly person like her work so hard. The old woman listened with surprising docility and it was agreed she would return to her own home. Though it was only midway through the month, Ishida gave her a full month's pay.

That evening the employment woman showed up again, accompanied by a maid to be hired on a trial basis. She was a young woman of 25 or 26, with thin hair. As she made her bow she turned her head to take a sidelong glance at Ishida's face. Some light-blue muslin forming the sleeve of her undershirt came out about an inch beyond the sleeve of her kimono.

The next day Ishida sent Shimamura to the employment agency and had him request a change of housemaids. This time a short girl of about sixteen with big, round eyes came. She looked like an energetic person, too. Ishida was favorably impressed with her.

After trying her for a few days, Ishida decided on keeping her. She was, she said, from Hinako; her name was Haru. She used boys' language in the Higo dialect, and her actions were also done with a boy's vigorousness. Her skin had an amber sheen, and her muscles were firm. "She's a little toughie," thought Ishida.

To his dismay, however, she always wore a brown-striped single-layer kimono that had patches on both

73

給仕をする。汗臭い。

「着物はそれしか無いのか。」

「ありまっせん。」

　平気で微笑を帯びて答える。石田は三枚持っている浴衣を一枚遣った。

　一週間程立った。春と一しょに泊まらせていた薄井の下女が暇を取って、師団長の内へ住み込んだ。春の給料が自分の給料の倍だというので、羨ましがって主人を取り替えたそうである。そこで薄井では、代に入れた分の下女を泊まりによこさないことになった。石田は口入れの上さんを呼んで、小女をもう一人雇いたいと言った。上さんが、そんなら内の娘をよこそうと言って帰った。

　口入れ屋の娘が来た。年は十三で久というのである。色の真っ黒な子で、頗る不潔で、頗る行儀が悪い。翌朝五時頃にぷっという妙な音がするので、石田は目を醒ました。後に聞けば、勝手では朝起きて戸を開けるまで、提灯に火を附けることにしている。提灯の柄の先に鉤が附いているのを、春はいつも長押の釘に懸けていたのだそうだ。その提灯を久に持っていろと言ったところが、久が面倒がって、提灯の柄で障子を突き破って、提灯を障子にぶら下げたということである。石田は障子に

knees. She served him at table with this same kimono on. It smelled of perspiration.

"Is that the only kimono you have?"

"Yes," she replied, without embarrassment and with a slight smile.

Ishida gave her one of the three yukata he had.

A week passed. The maid from Usui's place who had been staying overnight with Haru, quit and went to live in at the Division Commander's house. Ishida was told that she had said Haru's pay was twice as much as hers and so, to emulate Haru, she had changed masters. As a result, Usui refused to send his new replacement maid over to stay at Ishida's house. Ishida had the employment agency woman come again, and he told her he wanted to hire another girl.

"In that case I'll send my daughter," the woman said, and left.

The employment woman's daughter came. She was thirteen years old; her name was Hisa. Her skin was dark, very dark; she was terribly dirty; and her manners were terribly bad.

The next morning about five o'clock, Ishida was awakened by a strange ripping sound. When he inquired about it later, he was told that it was Haru's practice to light a lantern in the kitchen when she got up in the morning until she opened the shutters. She always hung the lantern from a peg in a crossbeam by means of a hook at the top end of its handle. She had given the lantern to Hisa to hold, but Hisa had felt it was too much of a bother and had shoved the handle of the lantern through a paper door and let the lantern dangle from the paper door. Ishida disliked having any holes

穴のあるのが嫌で、一々自分で切り張りをしているのだから、この話を聞いて嫌な顔をした。

石田は口入れ屋の上さんを呼んで、久を返したいと言った。返して代を雇う積であった。ところが、上さんは何が悪いか聞いて直させると言う。何一つ悪くないことのない子である。石田は窮して、なんにも悪くはない、女中は一人で好いと言った。

石田は達見に往って、第二の下女の傭聘を頼んだ。お上さんは狆をいじりながら、石田の話を聞いて、にやりにやり笑っている。そしてこう言うのである。

「あんたさん、立派なお妾でも置きなされればええにな。」

「馬鹿な事を言っちゃいかん。」

兎に角頼むと言い置いて、石田は帰った。しかし第二の下女はなかなか来ない。石田はとうとう若い下女一人を使っていることになった。

三四日立った。七月三十一日になった。朝起きて顔を洗いに出ると、春が雛の孵えたのを知らせた。石田は急いで顔を洗って台所へ出て見た。白い牝鶏の羽の間から、黄いろい雛の頭が覘いているのである。

商人が勘定を取りに来る日なので、旦那が帰ってから払うと言えと、言い置いて役所へ出た。午になって帰っ

in the paper doors and would patch each and every one by himself, so when he heard this account of what happened a look of great displeasure passed over his face.

He called for the employment agency woman and said he wanted to send Hisa back. He had intended to send her back and hire another, but then the woman said she wanted to hear what was wrong with her daughter so she could have her daughter correct it. There wasn't a thing that *wasn't* wrong with her. Ishida, hard pressed for a way out, said there was nothing wrong with her, all he needed was *one* servant girl.

Ishida then went to "Tatsumi" and asked the landlady there to arrange the engagement of a second servant girl. She grinned knowingly as she sat playing with her lapdog and listening to his story. Then she said, "What you, sir, ought to do is keep a nice mistress."

"Don't talk nonsense."

With one final request for her assistance, Ishida returned to his house. A second girl never came, however. Ishida ended up having only one young servant girl.

A few days passed. It was the 31st of July. When he rose in the morning and went to wash his face, Haru told him a chick had hatched. He washed his face quickly and went into the kitchen to see. Peeking out from between the white hen's feathers was the head of a yellow chick.

It was the day merchants came to settle accounts, so he told Haru to tell them the master would pay when he returned, and he left for the office. When he came

て見ると、待っているものもある。石田はノオトブック
にペンで書き留めて、片端から払った。

　晩になってから、石田は勘定を当って見た。小倉に来
てから、始めて纏まった一月間の費用を調べることが出
来るのである。春を呼んで、米はどうなっているかと問
うて見ると、丁度米櫃が空になって、跡は明日持って来
るのだと言う。そこで石田は春を勝手へ下がらせて、跡
で米の量を割って見た。陸軍で決めている一人一日精米
六合というのをはるかに超過している。石田は考えた。
自分はどうしても兵卒の食う半分も食わない。お時婆さ
んも春も兵卒ほど飯を食いそうにはない。石田は直にお
時婆さんの風呂敷包の事を思い出した。そして徐にノオ
トブックを将校行李の中へしまった。

　八月になって、司令部のものもてんでに休暇を取る。
師団長は家族を連れて、船小屋の温泉へ立たれた。石田
は纏まった休暇を貰わずに、隔日に休むことにしている。

　表庭の百日紅に、ぽつぽつ花が咲き始める。おりおり
蝉の声が向いの家の糸車の音にまじる。六日は日曜日
で、石田の所へも暑中見舞の客が沢山来た。初め世帯を
持つときに、澁紙のようなもので拵えた座布団を三枚
買った。まだ余り使わないのに中にいれた綿が方々に

back after noon, some were waiting for him. He jotted the figures down in a notebook with a pen and paid everything completely.

That evening he turned his attention to the accounts. This was the first time since coming to Kokura that he was able to study his expenses for a full month. He called Haru and asked her how the rice was. "The rice bin has just gone empty, and the next delivery will be tomorrow," she said. He sent her back to the kitchen and then calculated the amount of rice. He was using far in excess of the liter of polished rice the army allotted per person per day. He did some thinking. He himself certainly never ate even half what a private would eat. Neither the old woman Toki nor Haru seemed likely to eat as much as a private. Immediately he recalled the business about the old woman's *furoshiki* bundles. And very slowly he put the notebook back into his officer's traveling case.

In August the officers at headquarters each took holiday leave. The Division Commander left with his family for the hotsprings resort of Funagoya. Ishida was not given a continuous leave; he was able to stay home on alternate days.

A few flowers began to open on the crepe myrtle in the front garden. Occasionally the sounds of cicadas mixed with the sound of the spinning wheel across the street. The 6th being a Sunday, Ishida's place received numerous visitors paying their mid-summer courtesy calls. When he first moved in, he had bought three seatcushions made with something like tanned paper. Though they had hardly been used, the cotton stuffing

寄って塊になっている。客が三人までは座布団を敷かせることが出来るが、四人落ち合うと、畳んだ毛布の上に据わらせられる。今日なぞはとうとう毛布に乗ったお客があった。

客は大抵帷子に袴を穿いて、薄羽織を被て来る。薄羽織はもちろん、袴というものも石田なぞは持っていないのである。石田はこんな日には、朝から夏衣袴を着て応対する。

客は大抵同じような事を言って帰る。今年は暑が去年より軽いようだ。小倉は人気が悪くて、物価が高い。殊に家賃をはじめ、将校の階級によって価が違うのは不都合である。休暇を貰っても、こんな土地では日の暮らしようがない。町中に見る物はない。温泉場に行くにしても、二日市のような近い所は詰まらず、遠い所は不便で困る。先ずこんな事である。石田は只はあ、はあと返事をしている。

中には少し風流がって見る人もある。庭の方を見て、海が見えないのが遺憾だと言ったり、掛物を見て書画の話をしたりする。石田は床の間に、軍人に賜わった勅語を細字に書かせたのを懸けている。これを将校行李に入れてどこへでも持っていくばかりで、外に掛物というも

had formed uneven lumps all over. Thus he was able to set out these cushions for up to three visitors, but if four happened to come at the same time, one was made to sit on a folded blanket. On this particular Sunday, some visitors were finally forced to sit on blankets.

Most of the visitors were wearing thin jackets over summer upper garments and loose divided skirts. Now Ishida was the kind of person who did not own a divided skirt, let alone a thin jacket. On days like this when formal wear was called for, Ishida received visitors from the morning on wearing his summer uniform.

The visitors would generally say pretty much the same things and leave. "The summer this year is milder than last year's." "The general tone of Kokura is bad, and prices are high." "It's not fair the way prices vary depending on an officer's rank, especially the rent for a house." "Even if I get holiday leave what can I do during the day in a place like this? There's nothing to see anywhere in town." "Suppose you want to go to a hotsprings resort. Somewhere nearby, like Futsukaichi, is dull, while more distant places are too hard to get to." Et cetera, et cetera. Ishida would merely sit there and give polite Yes responses.

Some of the visitors tried to act a bit aesthetically inclined. Looking out towards the garden, they would say it's a shame the ocean couldn't be seen, or, looking at the scroll on the wall, they would talk about paintings and calligraphy. Ishida had hung in the tokonoma a scroll on which he had had the Imperial Precepts to Soldiers and Sailors written down in fine script. He kept it in his officer's traveling case and took it with him wherever he went; this was the only scroll he

のは持っていないのである。書画の話なんぞが出ると、自分には分らないと言って相手にならない。

翌日あたりから、石田も役所へ出掛けに、師団長、旅団長、師団の参謀長、歩兵の連隊長、それから都督と都督部参謀長との宅位に名刺を出して、それで暑中見舞を済ませた。

時候は段々暑くなって来る。蟬の声が、向いの家の糸車の音と同じように、絶間なく聞える。夕凪の日には、日が暮れてから暑くて内にいにくい。さすがの石田も浴衣に着更えてぶらぶらと出掛ける。初めのうちは小倉の町を知ろうと思って、ぐるぐる廻った。南の方は馬借から北方の果まで、北方には特科隊が置いてあるので、好く知っている。そこで東の方へ、船を砂の上に引き上げてある長浜の漁師村のはずれまで歩く。西の方へ、道普請に使う石炭屑が段々少くなって、天然の砂の現れてくる町を、西鍛冶屋町のはずれまで歩く。しまいには紫川の東の川口で、旭町という遊廓の裏手になっている、お台場の址が涼むには一番好いと決めて、材木の積んであるのに腰を掛けて、夕凪の蒸暑い盛りを過すことにした。

owned. Whenever the topic of painting or calligraphy came up, he would say he didn't know a thing about the subject and would take no part in the discussion.

The next day Ishida began visiting, on the way to his office, the homes of the Division Commander, the Brigade Commander, the Division Chief-of-Staff, the Infantry Regiment Commander, and finally the Governor-General and the Chief-of-Staff of the Governor-General's Section. In each place he took care of his mid-summer courtesy call by leaving his visiting card.

The weather gradually grew hotter. The cicadas buzzed as continually as the spinning wheel in the house across the street. On days when the wind died down in the evening, it was so hot after sunset that it was hard to stay indoors. Even Ishida gave in to changing to a yukata and going out for a stroll. At first, thinking he'd learn the various sections of Kokura, he covered the town in a circular pattern. On the south side he went from Bashaku to the farther end of Kitakata, which he already knew well because the technical corps was stationed there. Then he covered the eastern section, walking as far as the edge of the fishermen's village of Nagahama, where the boats were pulled up onto the sand. To the west he walked through a section where the coal tailings used for repairing roads gradually dwindled and the natural sand showed up, till he reached the edge of Nishi Kaji-machi. In the end he decided that the best place for cooling off was the ruins of the fort behind the licensed quarters of Asahi-machi, at the eastern mouth of the Murasaki River. There he would sit on a pile of lumber, waiting till the mugginess of the evening lull was past its peak.

そんな時には、今度東京に行ったら、三本足の床几を買って来て、ここへ持って来ようなんぞと思っている。

　孵えた雛は雌であった。至極丈夫で、見る見る大きくなる。大きくなるに連れて、羽の色が黒くなる。十日ばかりで全身真っ黒になってしまった。まるで鴉の子のようである。石田が捕まえようとすると、親鳥が鳴くので、石田は止めてしまう。

　十一日は陰暦の七夕の前日である。「笹は好しか」と言って歩く。翌日になって見ると、五色の紙に物を書いて、竹の枝に結び付けたのが、家毎に立ててある。小倉にはまだ乞巧奠の風俗が、一般に残っているのである。十五六日になると、「竹の花立は入りませんかな」と言って売って歩く。盂蘭盆が近いからである。

　十八日が陰暦の七月十三日である。百日紅の花の上に、雨が降ったり止んだりしている。向いの糸車は、相変らず鳴っているが、蝉の声は少しとぎれる。おりおり生垣の外を、跣足の子供が、「花柴々々」と呼びながら、走って通る。樒を売るのである。雨の止んでいる間は、ひどく蒸暑い。石田はこの夏中で一番暑い日のように感じた。翌日もやはり雨が降ったり止んだりして蒸暑い。夕方に町に出て見ると、どの家にも盆燈籠が点してある。

The thought occurred to him that, next time he went to Tokyo, he would buy a three-legged campstool and bring it along to this place.

The newly hatched chick was a female. Extremely healthy, it grew quickly. The bigger it grew the darker its feathers became. In ten days it was black all over. It looked just like a baby crow. Every time Ishida tried to catch it, the mother hen would let out a squawk, so he would give up.

The 11th was the eve of the Tanabata Festival according to the lunar calendar. Peddlers were about, asking, "Need any bamboo grass?" The next day, Ishida looked out to see paper of five different colors with writing on them, fastened to bamboo branches standing outside every single house. The custom of praying that their girls be skillful at handicrafts was still alive in Kokura. On the 15th and the 16th of the month, peddlers were calling out, "Bamboo vases for sale!" The Bon Festival was approaching.

The 18th was 13 July on the lunar calendar. It was raining on and off on the crepe myrtle flowers. The spinning wheel across the street hummed on as usual, but the buzzing of the cicadas was somewhat intermittent. Occasionally, barefoot children ran past the hedge fence calling out, "Flower bush, flower bush!" They were selling anise plants. During the pauses in the rain it was terribly muggy. Ishida thought it the hottest day that whole summer. The next day it was raining on and off and muggy again. When he went out into the streets that evening, there were Bon lanterns lit in every house.

中には二階を開け放して、数十の大燈籠を天井に隙間なく懸けている家がある。長浜村まで出て見れば、盆踊が始まっている。浜の砂の上に大きな圏を作って踊る。男も女も、手拭いの頬冠をして、着物の裾を片折って帯に挟んでいる。足袋はだしもあるが、多くは素足である。女で印袢纏に三尺帯を締めて、股引を穿かずにいるものもある。口々に口説というものを歌って、「えとさっさ」と囃す。好いとさの訛であろう。石田は暫く見ていて帰った。

雛は日にまし大きくなる。初めのうち油断なく庇っていた親鳥も、大きくなるに連れて構わなくなる。石田は雛を畳の上に持って来て米を遣る。段々馴れて手掌に載せた米を啄むようになる。また少し日が立って、石田が役所から帰って机の前に据わると、庭に遊んでいたのが、走って縁に上がって来て、鶴嘴を使うような工合に首をsagittaleの方向に規則正しく振り動かして、膝の傍に寄るようになる。石田は毎日役所から帰り掛けに、内が近くなると、雛の事を思い出すのである。

八月の末に、師団長は湯治場から帰られた。暑中休暇も残少なになった。二十九日には、土地のものが皆地蔵様へ詣るというので、石田も寺町へ往って見た。地蔵

Some of the houses had the second floor wide open with dozens of large lanterns hanging from the ceiling in a tight cluster. He went all the way to Nagahama, where he found the Bon dance had already begun. They were dancing in a huge circle on the sand of the beach. Men and women alike had their heads covered with hand towels tied under their chins, the hems of their yukatas tucked into their sashes. Some wore white *tabi*, but most were barefoot. A few of the women had on livery coats tied with cloth sashes, but wore no cotton pantaloons underneath. All were singing about the sexual escapades of a certain playboy, with the refrain "E to sassa." Ishida presumed this was dialect for "Yoi to sa." He watched for a while and went back home.

The chick grew bigger by the day. As it grew, even the mother hen, which in the beginning had protected it every minute, began to take no notice of it. Ishida would bring the chick up onto the straw-mat floor and give it some grains of rice. Gradually it grew tamer and even began to peck at grains of rice held in his palm. After a few days had passed, as soon as Ishida returned from work and sat in front of his desk, the chick would stop its play in the garden, come running up onto the verandah, and, rhythmically bobbing its head up and down in a pecking motion, come right up to his crossed legs. Every day on his way home, as soon as he was near the house Ishida would think of the chick.

At the end of August the Division Commander returned from the hotsprings resort. The summer holidays were almost over. On the 29th, because he heard that everyone in that region paid a visit to the god Jizō, Ishida also went to Tera-machi to have a look. In front

堂の前に盆燈籠の破れたのを懸け並べて、その真中に砂を山のように盛ってある。男も女も、線香に火を付けたのを持って来て、それを砂に立てて置いて帰る。

　中一日置いて三十一日には、又商人が債を取りに来る。石田が先月の通りに勘定をして見ると、米がやっぱり七月と同じように多く入っている。今月は風呂敷包を持ち出す婆さんはいなかったのである。石田は暫く考えて見たが、どうも春はお時婆さんのような事をしそうにはない。そこで春を呼んで、米が少し余計に入るようだがどう思うと問うて見た。

　春はくりくりした目で主人を見て笑っている。彼は米の多く入るのは当り前だと思うのである。彼は多く入るわけを知っているのである。しかしそのわけを言って好いかどうかと思って、暫く考えている。

　石田は春に面白い事を聞いた。それは別当の虎吉が、自分の米を主人の米櫃に一しょに入れて置くという事実である。虎吉の給料には食料が入っている。馬糧なんぞは余り馬を使わない司令部勤務をしているのに、定則だけの金を馬糧屋に払っているのだから虎吉が随分利益を見ているということを、石田は知っている。しかし馬さえ瘦せさせなければ好いと思って、あなぐろうとはし

of the Jizō Hall damaged Bon lanterns had been neatly ranged around a mound of sand heaped up high. Men and women brought burning incense sticks, which they would stand on end in the sand, then go home.

Two days later, on the 31st, the merchants once more came round to collect their bills. When Ishida made a calculation the way he had done the month before, he found that large quantities of rice had been consumed again, the same as in June. But this month there hadn't been any old woman carrying out *furoshiki*-wrapped bundles. He thought it over for a few minutes. No, Haru was not likely to do the sort of things old Toki did. So he called Haru and asked her what she thought, didn't it seem they were using a bit too much rice?

Haru looked at him with her big, round eyes and a smile on her lips. She thought it quite obvious why they were using a lot of rice. She knew the reason they used a lot. But for a few seconds she deliberated whether or not she should explain why.

Ishida was to learn a curious thing from Haru. It was that Torakichi, the stableman, was putting his rice into Ishida's rice bin, together with Ishida's rice. Now, Torakichi's wages included a food allowance. And Ishida was already aware of the fact that Torakichi was making a large profit on horse fodder, because, though Ishida was working at headquarters and therefore hardly used the horse, he nevertheless had been paying to the feed shop money for full quotas of fodder. But he hadn't bothered to look into the matter because he figured it was all right as long as Torakichi didn't let his horse lose weight. To take advantage of his master's le-

ない。そうしてあるのに、虎吉が主人の米櫃に米を入れて置くことにして、勝手に量り出して食うということに至っては、石田といえども驚かざることを得ない。虎吉は米櫃の中へ、米をいくら入れるか、何遍入れるか少しも分からないのである。そうして置いて、量り出す時にはいくらでも勝手に量り出すのである。段々春の言うのを聞いてみれば、味噌も醤油も同じ方法で食っている。内で漬ける漬物も、虎吉が「この大きい分は己の茄子だ」と言って出して食うということである。虎吉は食料は食料で取って、実際食うものは主人の物を食っているのである。春は笑ってこう言った。割木も別当さんのは「見せ割木」で、いつまで立っても減ることはないと言った。勝手道具もそうである。土間に七輪が二つ置いてある。春の来た時に別当が、「壊れているのは旦那ので、満足なのは己のだ」と言った。その内に壊れたのが丸で使えなくなったので、春は別当と同じ七輪で物を煮る。別当は、「旦那の事だから貸して上げるが、手めえはお辞儀をして使え」と言っているということである。

　石田は始めて目の開いたような心持ちがした。そして別当の手腕に対して、少なからぬ敬意を表せざることを得なかった。

niency, however, and go so far as to put his own rice into his master's bin and then take out and eat as much as he liked — why, even someone like Ishida couldn't help being shocked. Nobody would have the slightest idea how much rice Torakichi put in, or how often he put it in. In this arrangement, when he took it out, he would measure out as much as he liked. As Ishida listened to Haru's gradually unfolding tale, he learned that Torakichi was getting *miso* and soy sauce by the same method. Even Ishida's pickled vegetables Torakichi would take out for his own plate, saying, "These big ones here are *my* eggplants." Torakichi was taking money for his food allowance, but the things he was in fact eating were the master's things, Haru said with a smile. The stableman's firewood, too, was merely for show; the pile never went down. He was doing the same thing with the kitchen utensils. There were two portable charcoal stoves in the earth-floor area of the kitchen. When Haru came, the stableman told her, "The cracked one is the master's, the good one is mine." After a while the cracked one couldn't be used at all, so Haru was using the same charcoal stove for cooking as the stableman used. The stableman told her, she said, "Since it's for the master I'll let you use it, kid, but remember I'm only letting you use it as a favor."

Ishida felt as if his eyes had opened for the first time. At the same time, he couldn't help but greatly admire the stableman's cleverness.

　石田は鶏の事と卵の事を知っていた。知って黙許していた。然るに鶏と卵ばかりではない。別当には、systématiquementに発展させた、一種の面白い経理法があって、それを万事に適用しているのである。鶏を一しょに飼って、生んだ卵を皆自分で食うのは、唯このsystèmeを鶏に適用したに過ぎない。

　石田はこう思って、覚えず微笑んだ。春が、もし自分のこんな話をしたことが、別当に知られては困るというのを、石田はなだめて、心配するには及ばないと言った。

　石田は翌日米櫃やら、漬物桶やら、七輪やら、いろいろなものを島村に買い集めさせた。そして虎吉を呼んで、これまであった道具を、米櫃には米の入っているまま、漬物桶には漬物の入っているままで、みんな遣って、平気な顔をしてこう言った。

　「これまで米だの何だのが、お前のと一しょになっていたそうだが、あれは己が気が付かなかったのだ。己は新しい道具を買ったから、これまでの道具はお前に遣る。まだその外にもお前の物が台所に紛れ込んでいるなら、遠慮をせずに皆持って行ってくれい。それから鶏が四五羽いるが、あれは皆お前に遣るから、食うとも売るとも、勝手にするが好い。」

He had known about the chickens and the eggs and had been giving tacit consent to it. It wasn't only a matter of chickens and eggs, however. The stableman had an interesting method of economic management that he had developed systematically, and he was applying it to everything. Raising his hens together with Ishida's and then eating by himself all of the eggs that were laid was no more than applying the system to chickens.

As he thought of this he couldn't help smiling. Haru said she'd be in trouble if the stableman ever found out she had told the master all about him, but Ishida comforted her and told her there was nothing to worry about.

The next day Ishida had Shimamura buy a rice bin, a pickling tub, a portable charcoal stove, and various other things. Then he called Torakichi and gave him all the old utensils — the rice bin with all the rice in it and the pickling tub with all the pickled vegetables in it — and with a straight face said to him: "I'm told that up to now my rice and things have been together with yours; I hadn't been aware of that. I've bought some new utensils, so I'm giving you all the old ones. If any other things of yours are still mixed in with things in the kitchen, please don't hesitate to take them all away. And the four or five chickens that are around: I'm giving them all to you, you can eat them or sell them or do as you please with them."

　虎吉は呆れたような顔をして、石田の言うことを聞いていて、石田の詞が切れると、何か言いそうにした。石田はそれを言わせずにこう言った。

「いや。お前の都合はあるかも知れないが、己はそう決めたのだから、お前の話を聞かなくても好い。」

　石田はついと立って奥に入った。虎吉は春に、「旦那からお暇が出たのだかどうだか、伺ってくれろ」と頼んだ。石田は笑って、「己はそんな事は言わなかったと言え」と言った。

　その晩は二十六夜待だというので、旭町で花火が上がる。石田は表側の縁に立って、百日紅の薄黒い花の上で、花火の散るのを見ている。そこへ春が来て、こう言った。

「今別当さんが鶏を縛って持って行きよります。雛は置こうかと言いますが、置けと言いましょうか。」

「雛なんぞは入らんと言え。」

　石田はやはり花火を見ていた。

Torakichi listened to Ishida's words with a stunned expression on his face, and when Ishida finished speaking he started to say something. Ishida cut him off with, "No, it may be that other arrangements suit you better, but I've decided this is the way things will be and there's no need to hear what you have to say."

Ishida abruptly rose to his feet and went to his room. Torakichi asked Haru to please go ask the master if he'd been fired or what.

Ishida smiled. "Tell him I didn't say anything of the sort."

That evening was the Twenty-Sixth Night Festival, as it was called, and there was a fireworks display in Asahi-machi. Ishida was standing on the front verandah, watching fireworks exploding above the dark-gray blossoms of the crepe myrtle tree, when Haru came and said, "The stableman is tying up the chickens and taking them away. He wants to know if he should leave the chick. Should I tell him to leave it?"

"Tell him I don't need any chick."

And he turned back to watching the fireworks.